CELEBRATING

# *A Christ-Centered* CHRISTMAS

**Children's Edition**

A Family Nativity Tradition

Written by Emily Belle Freeman & David Butler ★ Illustrated by Ryan Jeppesen

ENSIGN PEAK

*To Kingston,*
*and each of the babies still to come.*
—EBF

*For Mom—who gifted me a spirit of radical giving*
*and the magic of Christmas.*
—DB

*For Kieth and Marianne—two of the most kind and*
*generous people I know. Next time dinner is on me.*
—RJ

text © 2017 Emily Belle Freeman and David Butler

illustrations © 2017 Ryan Jeppesen

All rights reserved. No part of this book may be reproduced in any form or by any means without permission in writing from the publisher, Ensign Peak®, at permissions@shadowmountain.com. The views expressed herein are the responsibility of the authors and do not necessarily represent the position of Ensign Peak.

Visit us at ShadowMountain.com

**Library of Congress Cataloging-in-Publication Data**
(CIP on file)
ISBN 978-1-62972-357-0

Printed in China
RR Donnelley, Shenzhen, China

10 9 8 7 6 5 4 3 2 1

Many, many years ago a young mother
started gathering Christmas traditions that would strengthen her
children's belief in Jesus Christ. Others who heard about the traditions wanted to
try them with their own children, so the young mother started writing them all down. It
wasn't long before that collection of Nativity traditions became a little book. After a while, the
mother's children grew up and moved away and started having babies of their own. The mother
wished she could teach her grandbabies to love the story of the night Jesus was born just as
her children did. So she gathered a few friends who loved Christmas as much as she did, and
together they wrote this children's edition of *Celebrating a Christ-Centered Christmas*.
The whimsical illustrations and colorful ornaments were created in hopes
that children everywhere would come to discover what it might
have been like to have been there

## on the night Jesus was born.

You can download the colorful ornaments, purchase that first little Christmas book, and discover other
Christ-centered celebrations your family will love at www.christcenteredcelebrations.com.

Luke 2:1,3

"And it came to pass in those days, that there went out a decree from Caesar Augustus, that all the world should be taxed. . . . And all went to be taxed, every one into his own city."

The sun was setting, and all was quiet except for the sound of hooves clip-clopping along the dusty trail. They had been walking for days—Mary, Joseph, and the donkey. Now they were almost to Bethlehem.

The place where the baby Jesus would be born.

Soon they would hold Him in their arms. They would open wide a space for Him in their hearts. But first, they had to find somewhere to stay. A quiet place.

They searched the whole city, but everyone they asked turned them away.

Until finally, someone offered Joseph and Mary a humble stable.

On the night Jesus was born,
**the innkeeper made room for Him.**

*Could you?*

How could you make room for the baby Jesus as part of your Christmas celebration this year?

On the First Night

Place an empty stable somewhere in your home where you can see it every day until Christmas.

# Joseph

### Luke 2:4–7

*"And Joseph also went up from Galilee, . . . unto the city of David, which is called Bethlehem; . . . to be taxed with Mary his espoused wife, being great with child. And so it was, that, while they were there, the days were accomplished that she should be delivered. And . . . there was no room for them in the inn."*

The stable was dark and dirty.
Even though he was tired, Joseph set to work clearing away the dung and sweeping away the dust. After searching for the cleanest straw, he prepared a soft place where Mary could rest. When he was finished, he hung a lantern in the doorway, and soft light blanketed the room.

All was calm, and all was bright.

On this holy night, Joseph's heartfelt desire was to make sure everything was ready for the miracle that was about to take place.

They were weary from the journey, strangers in a city far from home, but Joseph knew what to do.

On the night Jesus was born,
   **Joseph acted with kindness.**

*Could you?*

*Joseph*  If you had been there on the night Jesus was born, what would you have done to help get the stable ready?

*Joseph represents the desires of our hearts. He reminds us of the secret acts of Christmas kindness given with sacrifice and love to the broken, the weary, the lost, or the lonely.*

### On the Second Night

What secret act of Christmas kindness could your family participate in this season? As you perform your secret act, think of Joseph. His quiet acts went uncelebrated, but they were so needed. When you have finished this activity, place Joseph's figure in your waiting stable.

# Mary

Luke 2:6–7, 19

"And so it was, that, while they were there, the days were accomplished that she should be delivered. And she brought forth her firstborn son, and wrapped him in swaddling clothes, and laid him in a manger. . . . [And] Mary kept all these things, and pondered them in her heart."

The night was silent, and holiness filled the stable. After she finished counting tiny fingers and wrinkled baby toes, Mary tenderly wrapped her beautiful baby boy in clean swaddling cloth. Then she took Him into her arms. As she rocked Him, the young mother leaned close and kissed His soft cheek.

In the stillness of that evening, as she watched over her sleeping, swaddled son, Mary's heart filled with wonder. What would it be like to raise the Son of God? Jesus. The Savior of the world.

His birth was a miracle, but Mary knew without a doubt that it was only the beginning of the miracles to come.

On the night Jesus was born,
**Mary pondered all these things in her heart.**

*Could you?*

*Mary*  What do you think Mary pondered in her heart the night Jesus was born?

*Mary reminds us that we need to find a moment to ponder the events of that sacred night in Bethlehem. As we do this, we celebrate the miracle of Christ's birth and the gift heaven gave.*

### On the Third Night

Bake and decorate cookies as a family. During your time together, talk about the miracle of Christ's birth. Ponder how His birth has changed your life. When you have finished this activity, place Mary next to Joseph's figure in your waiting stable.

# Angels

### Luke 2:8–10, 13–14

"And there were in the same country shepherds abiding in the field, keeping watch over their flock by night. And, lo, the angel of the Lord came upon them, and the glory of the Lord shone round about them: and they were sore afraid.

And the angel said unto them, Fear not: for, behold, I bring you good tidings of great joy, which shall be to all people. . . .

And suddenly there was with the angel a multitude of the heavenly host praising God, and saying, Glory to God in the highest, and on earth peace, good will toward men."

The new star twinkled against the backdrop of darkness. A hush of stillness settled over the hillside, heavy with the anticipation of good things to come.

Suddenly, the night skies filled with hosts of angels, and the sound of their singing echoed through the hills. It was as if their hearts would burst with the great joy of the glad tidings they brought.

Christ the Lord had come. God's greatest gift. Their excitement overflowed from heaven.

On the night Jesus was born,
**Angels rejoiced.**

*Could you?*

*Angels*  Why do you think the birth of Jesus brought great joy?

*The Christ child reminds us to offer a gift to the Lord this Christmas season: a gift that is based on the true work of Christmas and that will allow us to focus on Christ all year long.*

### On the Seventh Night

Spend a quiet moment thinking about what your gift to Jesus could be. Choose one gift and write it down. Place it in a white envelope and put it somewhere for safekeeping until next year, when you can open and review it to remember your offering. When you have finished, place the baby Jesus figure in your waiting stable.